CHILDREN NEED
HEALTH CARE

Edwina Conner

THE WORLD'S CHILDREN

Children Need Education
Children Need Families
Children Need Food
Children Need A Future
Children Need Health Care
Children Need Homes
Children Need Recreation
Children Need Water

Series and Book Editor: Stephen White–Thomson
Designer: Ewing Paddock
Consultant: Save the Children
Picture Editor: Jane Marrow

All words that appear in **bold** in the text
are explained in the glossary on page 44.

First published in 1988 by
Wayland (Publishers) Limited
61 Western Road, Hove
East Sussex BN3 1JD, England

© Copyright 1988 Wayland (Publishers) Limited

British Library Cataloguing in Publication Data

Connor, Edwina
   Children need health care. – (The world's
children).
   1. Child health services
   I. Title   II. Series
   362.1'9892   RJ101

   ISBN 1–85210–106–7

Phototypeset by Kalligraphics Ltd, Redhill, Surrey
Printed in Italy by G. Canale & C.S.p.A., Turin
Bound by Casterman S.A., Belgium.

Title page: Healthy children enjoy their playtime
in a Sri Lankan school.

Contents page: On the streets of Calcutta it can be
hard work to keep healthy.

Front cover: These three Pakistani girls obviously
receive good health care.

Back cover: This Arab boy from Qatar looks the
picture of good health.

CONTENTS

THE RIGHTS OF THE CHILD

Eglantine Jebb, the founder of The Save the Children Fund, drafted the Rights of the Child in 1923. It was revised in 1948 by the present Declaration of the Rights of the Child, commonly known as the Declaration of Geneva. These principles form the basis of our work and the Charter of The Save the Children Fund.

1 The Child must be protected beyond and above all considerations of race, nationality or creed.

2 The Child must be cared for with due respect for the family as an entity.

3 The Child must be given the means requisite for its normal development, materially, morally and spiritually.

4 The Child that is hungry must be fed, the child that is sick must be nursed, the child that is mentally or physically handicapped must be helped, the maladjusted child must be re-educated, the orphan and the waif must be sheltered and succoured.

5 The Child must be the first to receive relief in time of distress.

6 The Child must enjoy the full benefits provided by social welfare and social security schemes, must receive a training which will enable it, at the right time, to earn a livelihood, and must be protected against every form of exploitation.

7 The Child must be brought up in the consciousness that its talents must be devoted to the service of its fellow men.

BUCKINGHAM PALACE

All children, regardless of race, nationality or creed, have basic rights. These rights were outlined by Eglantine Jebb, the founder of Save the Children, in 1923 and they have now become an integral part of the United Nations charter. You can read them on the opposite page.

I welcome this thought-provoking series and applaud the way it confronts the issues facing today's children throughout the world. In the end we are all part of the same human race, and not so different from one another. Where differences do exist, they enrich us.

As Britain's largest international children's charity, Save the Children works where there is real need, both in the UK and in over 50 countries around the world. The idea behind all our projects is to encourage people to help themselves. But SCF also accepts its responsibility to talk about the issues of world-wide child poverty - particularly to the young - which makes this work so necessary. This series is designed to do just that.

I am sure that this colourful series will be an invaluable resource for any school whose aim is to make their pupils think beyond the confines of their playground and their community. We are one world after all. Let's try and be one.

Anne

HEALTH EQUALS HAPPINESS

What do you think is the most important thing in life? Plenty of money? A good job? Fame? A holiday abroad every year?

All these things are attractive of course, but without good health it's impossible to enjoy them. Izaak Walton (1593–1683), author of a book called *The Compleat Angler*, once said that health 'is a blessing that money cannot buy.' Ill health stops you doing what you want to do. That is the case all over the world, in rich countries as well as poor countries.

Some children living in parts of Africa or Asia, where there is not always enough to eat, battle to stay alive. An attack of measles or diarrhoea can kill children who are weak from hunger.

Living in a **developed country**, such as Australia, France or Britain, does not stop people becoming ill, but the illnesses are different. The biggest killer in developed countries is heart disease. Many children and adults in Western countries also suffer from cancer, arthritis or asthma. Others are physically handicapped or mentally ill.

The importance of keeping healthy and the need to fight disease are the same all over the world. Some countries, such as Sweden, and the African countries of Mozambique and Zimbabwe, spend money on providing free health care.

Keeping fit and taking exercise are important ways of staying healthy. ▽

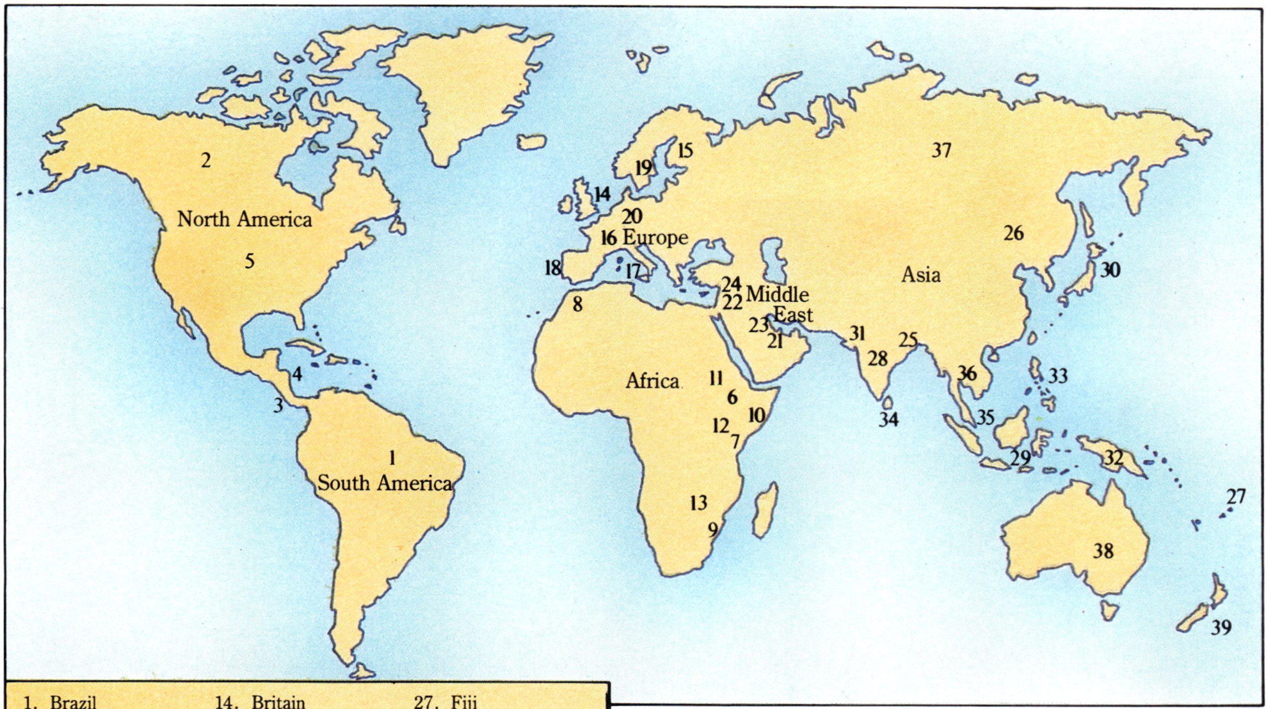

A map of the world to help you find the places mentioned in this book.

1.	Brazil	14.	Britain	27.	Fiji
2.	Canada	15.	Finland	28.	India
3.	Costa Rica	16.	France	29.	Indonesia
4.	Honduras	17.	Italy	30.	Japan
5.	USA	18.	Portugal	31.	Pakistan
6.	Ethiopia	19.	Sweden	32.	Papua New Guinea
7.	Kenya	20.	West Germany	33.	Philippines
8.	Morocco	21.	Bahrain	34.	Sri Lanka
9.	Mozambique	22.	Jordan	35.	Singapore
10.	Somalia	23.	Kuwait	36.	Thailand
11.	Sudan	24.	Lebanon	37.	USSR
12.	Uganda	25.	Bangladesh	38.	Australia
13.	Zimbabwe	26.	China	39.	New Zealand

Health equals happiness all over the world. It's up to governments to make sure that these Ethiopian children, and children everywhere, have access to good health care and know enough about hygiene and disease to look after themselves. ▽

In other countries, however, such as the USA, health care is good but you have to pay for it. Poor people cannot afford the best treatment, so even though there are plenty of doctors and medicine available, not everyone gets the care they need.

We must, of course, have doctors and hospitals to treat disease, but keeping healthy is everyone's responsibility. It is up to all of us to help those less fortunate than ourselves. In this book we shall look at some of the causes of ill health, how it can be prevented, how it is treated in different parts of the world and how people everywhere are learning to look after themselves.

OUR BODIES' DEFENCES

The body is a complicated and clever machine that knows how to look after itself. It has thousands of working parts and special feeding systems to keep it going. If anything goes wrong, a defending army with all kinds of weapons marches in to renew dead cells, help skin grow again, heal cuts and broken bones, and fight germs.

But if our bodies' defences cannot cope with an attack, we become ill. Many illnesses are caused by tiny germs living off food in cells which keep us healthy. So we feel ill until our defences, known as our **immune system**, have killed all the germs.

There are many other reasons why people become ill. If something goes wrong with the circulation of the blood, for example, a heart attack might occur. Cancers are caused when faulty cells in the body multiply and destroy healthy cells. Many cancers can now be cured if diagnosed in the early stages.

AIDS (Acquired Immune Deficiency Syndrome) is an incurable disease which attacks the immune systems, and so the body cannot resist infection. The AIDS virus is transmitted in its strongest form in blood and, before it was identified, people became infected because they had blood transfusions. People who have had many sexual partners and drug addicts who share needles to inject drugs are in greatest danger of becoming infected.

Other diseases, such as **haemophilia**, are acquired at birth. Haemophilia is carried by women, but only male children inherit it from their mothers.

Some illnesses are caused when the wrong medicine is given to a patient, or when a medicine has an unknown side-effect. In 1961 a drug called thalidomide was taken off the market. It had been given to pregnant women with 'morning sickness' who, after treatment, gave birth to malformed babies.

When people do not get enough food they suffer from **malnutrition**. Without food, the body cannot grow properly and cannot fight infection. Malnourished people in poor countries become ill. In rich countries illness can be caused by overeating. People who are very fat run a serious risk of getting high **blood pressure** and heart problems, but, unlike people in **developing countries**, they can choose to lead healthier lives.

△ The Chinese take their exercises very seriously. At this elementary school in Guangzhou, physical exercise is part of the daily routine. Experts think regular exercise helps protect the body against heart disease.

◁ Alexei, son of the Tsar of Russia, suffered from haemophilia. In this disease, the blood does not clot properly, so that small cuts can be dangerous and internal bleeding very likely. Only boys get haemophilia.

The body is very good at healing itself. This little girl has broken her arm. If she leaves it in plaster for six weeks or so, the bone will mend and it will be as good as new. ▷

HOW HEALTHY IS THE WORLD?

The world is a healthier place than it was 100 years ago. People are living longer. Fewer babies and children are dying. This is partly because doctors know more about diseases and how they can be cured. Nowadays, hospitals use modern, highly-sophisticated technology to treat cancers, heart problems and other killer diseases.

Learning how to prevent illness is as important for the world's health as any scientific discoveries. Providing clean water, teaching people how to look after themselves, caring properly for pregnant women and their babies, all help the world's population live healthier and longer lives. Smallpox, which once killed millions of people, has been wiped out because so many people were immunised against the disease. Although we can now save thousands of lives with **heart transplants** and by-pass operations, the numbers of deaths from other illnesses are shocking.

In 1986, UNICEF (United Nations Children's Fund) published a detailed report. It stated that three million children under five died of malaria, two million died of measles and five million died from the effects of diarrhoea.

In general, public health and health education are improving, but there are still many problems, and more work to be done.

Yes, people are living longer, but they live longer in some countries than in others. While people in France or Germany or the USA can expect to live to over 70 years of age, in South-east Asia the average life span is only 59 years, and in Africa it is 51 years.

But the developed world has its own health problems. A 1987 report in Britain showed that while rich people are getting healthier, poorer people are becoming less healthy. Unemployment, poverty and bad housing result in a poor diet and more sickness. At the same time, doctors' **prescription charges** are going up, doctors in poorer areas are overworked and hospital services are overstretched. So, in Britain at the moment, as in developing countries, when more people need good health care, it is less likely that they are going to get it.

◁ **Gradually, killer diseases such as measles are being brought under control. But there is much work to be done if more children are to grow up happy and healthy, like these schoolchildren in north Mozambique.**

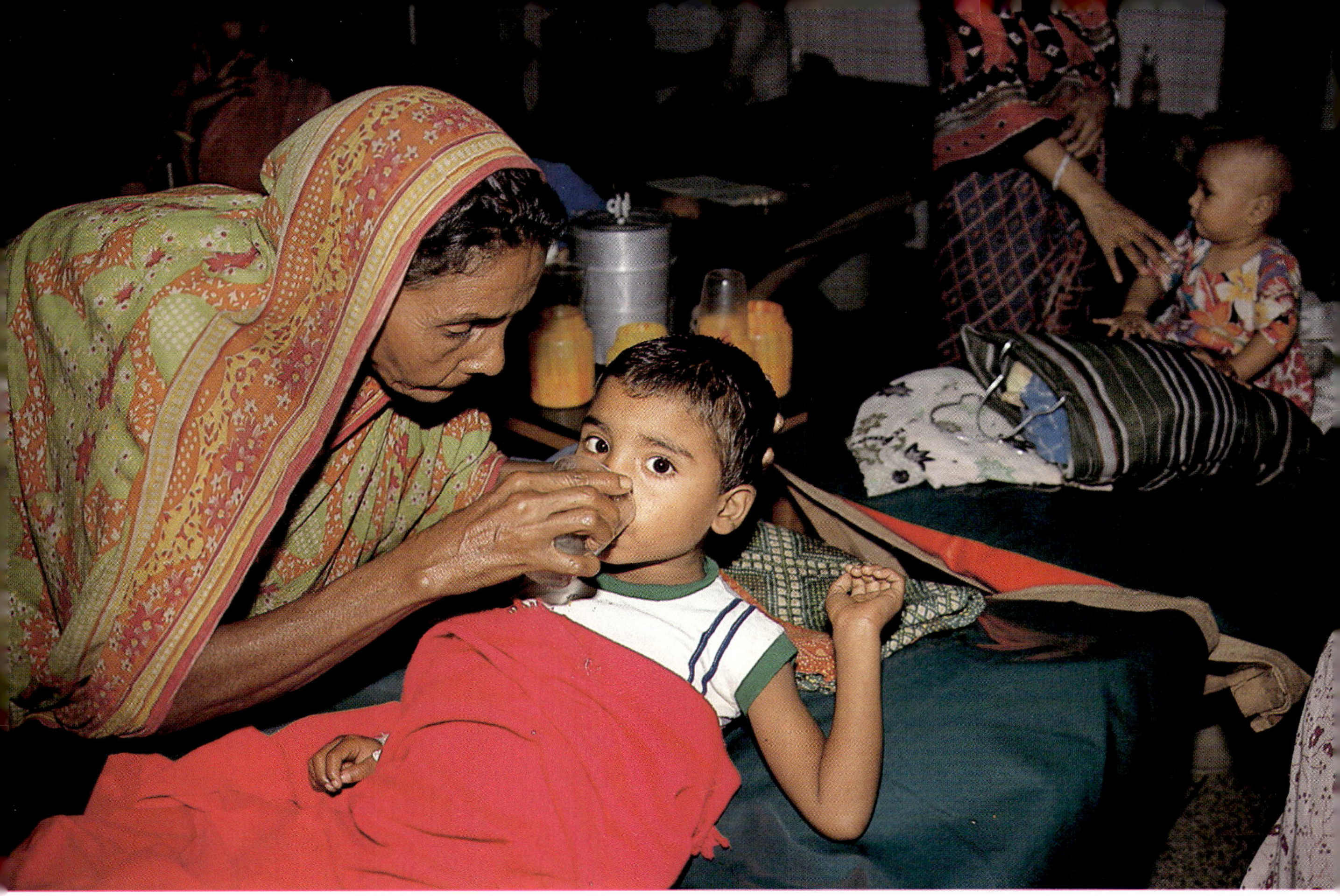

△ Young children often contract diarrhoea after eating contaminated food or water. It's not necessary to give them expensive medicines, but they must drink plenty of fluids or they will become dehydrated and could die.

Many diseases, such as smallpox, have been wiped out because of widespread immunisation. Researchers are constantly working to find out more about diseases. This is a laboratory in a Bangladesh hospital. ▷

POVERTY

If people are very poor, they find it hard to stay healthy. Anyone with a decent place to live and enough money to buy food, is likely to be more healthy than someone less fortunate.

In Western countries, such as the USA or Britain, many families on low incomes, or who live on **social security**, have to put up with damp and overcrowded living conditions. Poor housing can affect health, leading to serious chest problems, such as pneumonia or bronchitis, particularly in small children. As a result, parents become depressed and worry about the future of their family.

Worldwide, over 100 million people have no roof over their heads at all. In Asia, for example, there are nearly 84 million children living in extreme poverty. In many cities in the developing world half the inhabitants live in slums, without lavatories or running water, always at risk of disease.

Many of the poor in Africa are **refugees**. They have had to leave their homes because of war or famine and start life again somewhere else. Most of them have no money, no work, no food and few possessions. They are weak and, unless they receive help quickly, some children may die of **dehydration** from having diarrhoea or malnutrition. Help does not always reach everyone in time.

No one need go hungry because there is enough food to feed everyone in the world, and no one should die of simple illnesses because there is enough money to pay for good health care. But some countries eat more food than they need and do not do enough to help poor countries help themselves.

Many developing countries are forced to use some of their best land to grow tea or tobacco for export, rather than to grow food crops for themselves. They need to sell products like these to rich countries so that they can buy essentials for themselves, such as oil and machinery. Unfortunately, they are not always paid fairly for these things, and are forced into borrowing money from rich countries and then into paying it back when they cannot afford it.

All these wrongs must be put right if we want to stop children dying and watch them grow up strong and healthy.

◁ **In both developed, and developing, countries thousands of people have nowhere to live. Many families, like this one in Calcutta, India, simply live on the streets with no shelter and no privacy.**

△ The 1987 International Year for Shelter for the Homeless aimed to improve housing conditions all over the world. No one should have to live in dirty, damp homes like this one in Britain. To do so is depressing and can lead to severe health problems.

◁ The unemployment rate in the United States, as in Europe, is too high. Without a job it is very hard to afford a home – this man's home in Florida, USA, is his supermarket trolley; and without a home it is hard to settle down in a job.

DIET

We are what we eat – have you heard that expression? We have to eat to live: every part of our body – muscles, bones, blood, all the organs – needs food. We need good, balanced meals to grow up strong and healthy.

In the developing world there is not always enough food to go round, and one disaster can spell death and disease for thousands of children and their parents. Over the last few years this has happened in African countries like Ethiopia, the Sudan and Mozambique.

In the Philippine Islands, sugar cane is the most important export crop. But when the world price of sugar slumped in the early 1980s, the economy of the Philippines was badly hit and, by 1985,

over 40 per cent of children under 14 were underfed. Families could not afford one meal of rice and vegetables a day. At this point local health workers and UNICEF began teaching parents about health and nutrition. They showed children basic gardening techniques, so that in the future people would understand the importance of growing enough food to feed themselves, if they have the land to do so.

But it's not just people in poor countries who have a bad diet. There is no shortage of food in developed countries, but this does not mean that people eat a healthy diet. Experts have found that young teenagers, particularly girls, lack important minerals and

◁ **The Chinese diet consists mainly of rice, vegetables and fish. If there is plenty of it, it is healthier than a Western diet which is full of fat, sugar and salt. Nevertheless, in many parts of Asia, there are thousands of undernourished children.**

These children are tucking into a favourite British meal that is full of fat and salt – fried fish and chips. An unvaried diet like this could mean they'll develop heart disease later in life and become fat and unhealthy. ▷

vitamins, especially iron, which is found in green vegetables. This is because they eat too much **'junk' food** – chips, tomato ketchup, cans of lemonade, for example – which contain plenty of fat or sugar but not much dietary fibre.

Dietary fibre is found in all plants. It is the skeleton of a plant, and is an important part of a healthy diet. Studies of other people whose diet is rich in fibre, show that eating fibre regularly reduces the risk of diseases of the bowel later in life. A junk diet which could lead to high blood pressure and heart disease should be replaced with a diet which includes more wholemeal bread and cereals, fresh fruit, fish and vegetables, and less red meat, fat, sugar and salt.

△ **During the Ethiopian famine, many children died before help could get to them. This baby was lucky. She is being given a special high-protein meal to boost her weight quickly and protect her against disease.**

WATER PROBLEMS

Water is essential to life and health. We need it to drink, to cook, and to wash ourselves and our clothes. Without clean water, staying healthy is almost impossible.

If you live in a town or city in the industrialized world and you want a glass of water or a hot bath, you just turn on a tap. Water is piped to buildings through a complicated underground system, and is usually treated with chemicals to make it safe to drink. If this treatment fails then people can become ill. Hepatitis, typhoid, amoebic dysentery and cholera are all serious diseases caused by drinking **contaminated** water. In parts of Portugal, for instance, it is not safe to drink tap water because it is not properly treated.

Piping water from rivers or wells to remote villages in some parts of the developing world is difficult and expensive. Fetching water from a well is usually a job for women who may have to travel several miles twice a day to fill up a heavy pitcher and walk home again. Unless special care is taken, the water in the well may become dirty because dust, rubbish or animal dung fall into it.

It's easy to see how poor sewage and drainage can lead to disease in this Bangladesh village. ▽

△ **Factories and power stations pumping out contaminated waste matter into this Italian river pollute the water and make it unfit for drinking.**

In a severe drought, rivers, lakes and ponds dry up. There is no water to be had anywhere and without water, animals and people die, and crops fail. ▷

So you can see that keeping clean, preparing food and getting enough to drink is hard work.

The Mediterranean Sea is very **polluted** because so much rubbish from factories and sewage has been dumped in it. In some areas it is dangerous to swallow the water or eat the local seafood which may be contaminated with dangerous chemicals.

Sometimes a country has a drought, when no rain falls for a very long time. Wells, rivers and even **reservoirs** dry up. During the hot summer of 1976 in Britain, the supply of water to people's homes had to be turned off at local waterworks for several hours a day to save water. A drought in a very hot country is more serious. Without water crops cannot grow, animals die and people starve.

On page 25 you can read about projects to supply clean drinking water to people who badly need it.

POOR HEALTH CARE

Every year throughout the world 14.5 million babies and children under five years old die. This figure would be reduced if more women expecting babies had regular medical check-ups and ate the extra vitamins needed during pregnancy. If the mother is not eating well, a baby does not grow properly and will be born underweight and weak. Weak babies may die of an infection, and unfit mothers may become ill and die having just given birth.

Experts in Europe have been studying Sudden Infant Death Syndrome or 'cot death'. Babies who seem to be perfectly healthy die suddenly in their sleep. These deaths seem to be linked to poor living conditions, which have led to general ill health in a family.

In some countries mother and child health care is good. In Japan, Singapore and Finland, few babies and children now die. But in Somalia, for every 1,000 babies born alive, 152 die in their first year. Baby deaths could be prevented if governments would spend more money on health education. Unfortunately, many in the developing world cannot afford to do so. More clinics are needed so that health workers can show mothers how to look after themselves and their babies, and how important it is to do so. Babies need to be immunised against diseases too.

△ **A family planning poster in India, urging people to have fewer children.**

◁ **A health care clinic in Somalia.**

A health visitor checking out a new-born baby in El Salvador. ▽

In the developed world, starting a family is an important decision, especially for a woman. In developing countries the pressures are different. **Contraception** – preventing a woman becoming pregnant – is very important, but it canot be forced on families. When parents know their children might die, they want to have more babies, in the hope that perhaps one or two of them will live. But if a mother in these circumstances has two or three children under five years old, it is likely that one of them will become seriously malnourished.

It is only when better care is available and parents believe their babies will live, that they will think about family planning.

On page 30 you can read about some mother and baby health care projects in different parts of the world.

DANGER ALL AROUND

Our health is affected by our environment. In Hunza in Pakistan, for example, people live to a great age. There are no factories to pollute the air or the fresh water from the mountains. The land is fertile, so food is fresh and there is plenty of it. The people have a healthy diet.

Unfortunately, this ideal situation does not exist worldwide. Our environment is threatened all the time by our own actions, from spraying our crops with dangerous chemicals to nuclear accidents. In 1986 an explosion at a nuclear power station in Chernobyl, USSR, killed many people. Some who were close by contracted **radiation sickness**, others will become ill later in their lives. Farm land was contaminated, not only in the USSR but also in Western Europe because the winds carried the radiation westwards.

Safety checks are essential in dangerous industries to avoid serious disasters. In 1984 in Bhopal, India, poisonous gas escaped from a chemical factory and the people who lived nearby became very ill. Many were permanently injured and many died.

Conditions at work can cause illness too. For example, many coal miners get lung diseases from breathing in coal dust.

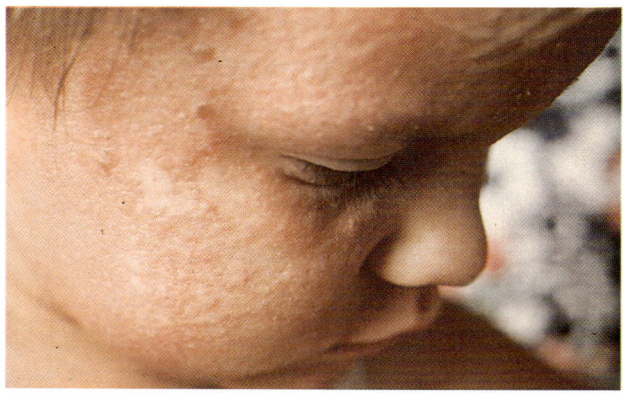

△ Sometimes poisonous gas or chemicals escape from a factory or power station. The effects on people living nearby can be devastating. This child lived in Soweso, Italy, when just such a tragedy occurred. Her face is badly scarred.

◁ In parts of the world where there is little pollution, people live to be very old. This family are from the mountains of Pakistan.

△ Scientists check the radiation level in the fields around Chernobyl, in the USSR, after the nuclear explosion in 1986.

In some parts of the world children are affected too. They often do adult work, either to learn skills that will be useful to them when they grow up, or perhaps because their families need the extra money. In Thailand, for example, 10,000 children a year are sold by their families to work in factories for very little money. They are not looked after properly and become ill.

Laws to protect children are often ignored. The USA has passed many laws to stop children working, but even so, almost a quarter of people working on American farms are children. Many of them are hurt in accidents. In the USA, an 11 year-old boy, Michele Colenna, committed suicide after he was sent by his family to work on a farm where he was treated badly.

Children should not do adult work. They are not as strong as adults. Some **voluntary organizations** now help schoolchildren learn how to farm or build so they do not have to work to learn these skills. This is happening in Zambia, Tanzania and Indonesia and so fewer children in these countries are working long, hard hours.

LIFESTYLE

What we eat certainly affects our health, and so does the way we live. People who smoke tobacco know they risk dying of lung cancer or other diseases. Drinking alcohol can cause liver disease, and a pregnant woman who drinks too much alcohol may harm her unborn baby. Drugs such as heroin and cocaine are extremely dangerous. They affect the body and the mind and can kill. If we choose not to drink, smoke or take drugs it means we are less likely to become ill.

Our health is also affected by **stress** and anxiety. Stress has many causes such as too much work, illness, divorce, buying and selling a house, the effects of unemployment or worrying about money.

Children as well as adults are affected by stress. This may be caused by arguments at home, worrying about other family difficulties, the fear of nuclear war or the fact that they may not get a good job when they leave school.

Sometimes the pressures on teenagers to escape their problems by taking drugs are very great.

Unfortunately, an unhealthy lifestyle can make stress and depression worse. Keeping fit and looking after our bodies helps us cope with our problems. It is not enough just to avoid cigarettes and alcohol and drugs, we need to do something more positive. This means taking exercise and getting enough sleep and relaxation too. A recent report shows that many children in the developed world are overweight, take no exercise and get tired running just a few metres. A shocking state of affairs!

As you can see on page 28, when given the opportunity, children in poorer countries happily take resonsibility for keeping themselves healthy, and help their families too. This is a lesson we should all learn if we want to live longer and healthier lives.

Drinking and smoking are popular pastimes, but too much of either can lead to bad health. ▽

Some children start to smoke very young. Once they've started it's very hard to give up. ▽

These Americans keep fit by roller skating. Taking exercise regularly helps the heart to work properly and protects it against disease.

A BETTER PLACE TO LIVE

When Britain's Queen Victoria came to the throne in 1837, London was very dirty. Big factories belched out harmful smoke and soot. There was no proper water supply or sewage system, and rubbish was not collected regularly. The streets were busy and dirty. The River Thames was polluted, smelly and its banks were a good home for rats. Many people died of cholera and other diseases.

Gradually these problems were put right. With clean water and a proper sewage system, public health improved.

It is the same story all over the world. When people have clean water and are able to keep their homes and streets clear of rubbish and sewage, they become healthier.

1987 was International Year for Shelter for the Homeless. Many organizations in different countries

Taking clean water to an outlying village can be a major problem, involving miles of pipeline. Everyone has to cooperate if such a project is going to succeed. This pipe is in Somalia and has improved living conditions for the local people. ▽

promised to help build new and better homes for people, providing a proper water supply and toilet for every house or group of houses. Volunteers in Sri Lanka are helping Tamil refugees build their own homes and dig a well to provide clean water.

Children in villages in Honduras were longing to have taps in their houses. Their parents wanted clean water to drink and cook with, and to water their vegetable gardens. The Canadian International Development Agency and Save the Children put some money into a project for clean water for some of these villages.

It was hard work. The clean water source was a long way from the villages, and the ground in between was rocky. Local people had to dig the trench to carry the pipes. Then the source had to be sealed off to keep it unpolluted, and the water stored in a tank near the village. With water, toilets and showers can be built, the children can be taught hygiene and vegetables can be grown. All this adds up to a better diet, healthier lives and produce to sell.

In Honduras, as in Ethiopia or the Sudan, or the poorer parts of some European countries, improved public health is the key to a better life for many families.

This is a scheme in Nairobi, Kenya, to rehouse people living in slums. The houses are clean and there is a sewage system and water supply. ▽

IMMUNISATION

Some diseases can be prevented by immunisation. This is done by injecting people with a special mixture of drugs which stop them getting ill. Smallpox used to be a deadly disease. Nowadays no one gets it because a **vaccine** stopped it from spreading.

Vaccinating children saves lives. In the developing world, children die of diseases that are not serious in the developed world. Measles is an example. In 1985, over two million children in poorer countries died of measles. They caught the disease because they had not been immunised. They died because their bodies were weak from lack of food and they were unable to fight the infection.

In Western countries children who get measles do not usually die, although they used to. About 60 years ago there was a serious **epidemic** of measles in Glasgow.

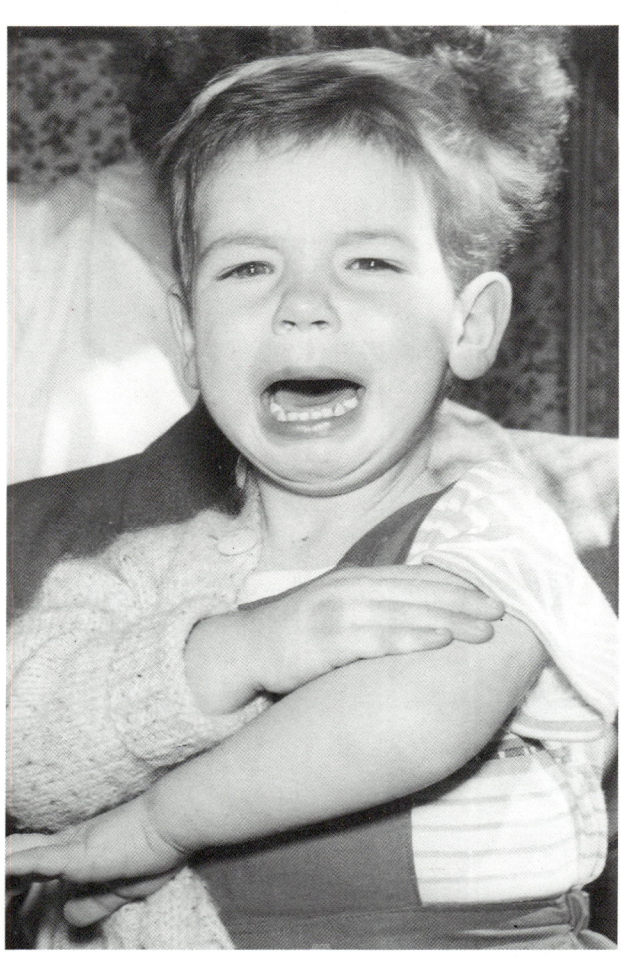

△ **Children everywhere must be vaccinated against diseases which can kill. Polio, measles, tetanus, whooping cough and TB are still dangerous and, once they appear in a community, can spread very quickly, especially among babies and toddlers.**

◁ **This is a health clinic in Karachi, Pakistan, where hundreds of mothers bring their babies to be weighed and immunised against disease. One of the problems is getting the information about the clinic and about the importance of vaccination to families. Health workers try to visit as many homes as possible, explaining how the clinic can keep their children healthy.**

△ The smallpox vaccine was prepared from the sores of a disease called Cowpox which affected cows. This cartoon, drawn in 1802, shows that the idea was not taken completely seriously at first!

Glasgow is a big city in Scotland. One child in 20 died. Nowadays, children are immunised against measles at an early age. TB, polio, diphtheria, tetanus and whooping cough can also be prevented by immunisation. They are serious diseases, but no one in the world today should die of them.

Immunisation works wonders, but for those in developing countries there are lots of problems.
● Vaccines cost money.
● Getting the vaccines to the right places is difficult and expensive when roads are bad or flooded.
● Explaining to families in countries where many cannot read and few have a radio or TV, *why, when* and *where* to take their children to be immunised takes a lot of helpers a long time.
● A mother may have to give up half a day's wages when she takes her child to the health centre some kilometres away.
● Some vaccines, such as the one for polio, have to be kept cold or they will not work. This is expensive in hot countries.

But there is good news, too. Health workers in many countries are being helped by their governments and by organizations such as Save the Children and UNICEF to vaccinate more and more children. Every year more lives are saved.

TEACHING HEALTH

Doctors, hospitals and drugs are important if diseases are to be cured. But more important is teaching people how to keep themselves well. This is called 'preventive' medicine. If rich countries want to stop people dying of cancer and heart disease, more money must be put into health education.

In Britain, as well as in other developed countries, primary school children are taught about the dangers of smoking, drinking alcohol and eating junk food. In the 1980s children are also learning how to protect themselves against the new disease, AIDS.

Many people in the world cannot get to doctors when they need to, so they must learn about hygiene, diet, first aid and how to treat simple illnesses. Health workers and villagers in many developing countries work together until people understand how to improve their own health.

Some medicines are essential, but others sold to developing countries by rich drug companies are not. A mother should know that if her baby has diarrhoea, she does not need expensive **antibiotics**. The best treatment is ORT (oral rehydration therapy) to stop the baby becoming dehydrated. This means giving the baby doses of boiled water with a mixture of sugar and salt.

Child-to-Child is a scheme working in over one hundred countries. In many poor areas, younger children are looked after by older brothers and sisters, so teachers

△ **Indian health workers show local people how to look after themselves and protect themselves against disease. Many people cannot get to a doctor easily and their knowledge of hygiene and first aid could be life-saving in an emergency.**

and health workers show the older children how to look after babies and toddlers, as well as the rest of the family. They learn how to give ORT and to check eyesight, hearing and weight. They also take babies to be vaccinated against disease.

△ Dental caries (tooth decay) affects children everywhere. Avoiding sweets is a good idea, and cleaning your teeth properly is very important. These children are learning how it's done.

In many parts of the world, older children have to take responsibility for their younger brothers and sisters. Many are taught how to keep an eye on their family's health. ▽

In Pune, India, people are still dying of leprosy, a very contagious skin disease. Children learn how to spot the first signs and report the case to a health clinic. All these children are responsible health workers.

In Papua New Guinea, Save the Children is working with communities needing more variety in their diets. They are now growing beans and peanuts on their own allotments.

Preventive medicine works. It is the best way to save lives all over the world.

CHILD CARE

We have seen on page 18 that far too many babies and young children die. But in spite of the problems caused by poverty, most countries are working hard to improve the care of mothers and children.

In Sri Lanka, China, Costa Rica and Thailand, for instance, far fewer babies die now than 20 years ago. In Algeria the government has put money into health education and aims to halve the number of baby and child deaths before the end of the 1980s. They hope that all children will soon be vaccinated against measles, diphtheria, whooping cough and tetanus. They are retraining over 30,000 health workers to care for mothers and children in particular.

Uganda is an African country suffering from the effects of war and drought. Health centres have been destroyed and so many children have not been vaccinated. But now health workers helped by Save the Children and UNICEF are making huge efforts to reach every family. They explain how parents can treat diarrhoea, and how important it is for mother to immunise their babies and check their weight and growth regularly. They talk to schools, and go to church, youth and women's organizations, delivering pamphlets and posters. Loudspeaker vans in the streets, and radio and TV broadcasts put the message across to people who cannot read. The government hopes that 90 per cent of children in the cities, and at least half of children living outside the cities,

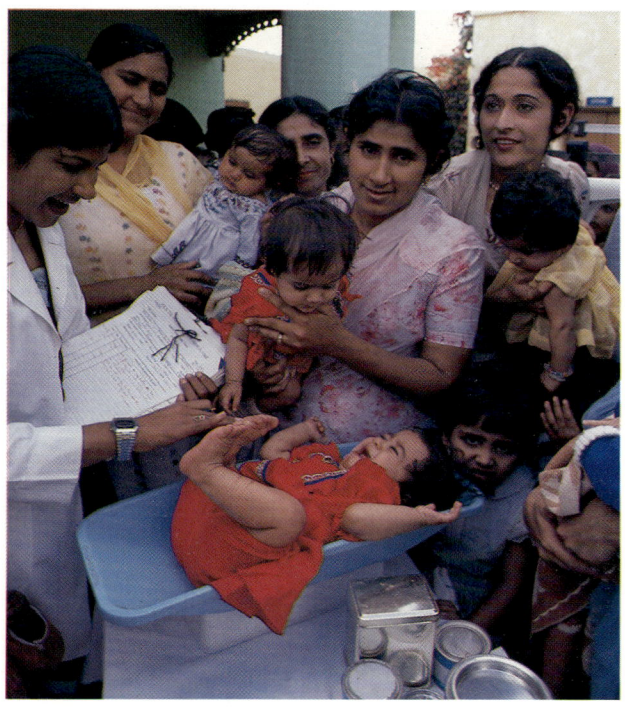

△ **A health clinic often provides a place for** mothers to meet to chat about their problems and their children's health. The more people who attend the clinics, the better health workers can spread understanding of disease and how to avoid it.

will soon be immunised. This is becoming a great success story.

Public housing policies in the USA and Britain have often led to the isolation of families on large estates. Save the Children believe poor living conditions can lead to poor health. Their Riverside Child Health Project in Newcastle, England, helps parents to meet and talk together about health issues. It also encourages Health Service staff to find better ways of working with families who are on low incomes.

△ Vast, impersonal housing estates, with nowhere to play or meet your friends, can be isolating and depressing and can lead to health problems. Community projects where people can meet and talk do help.

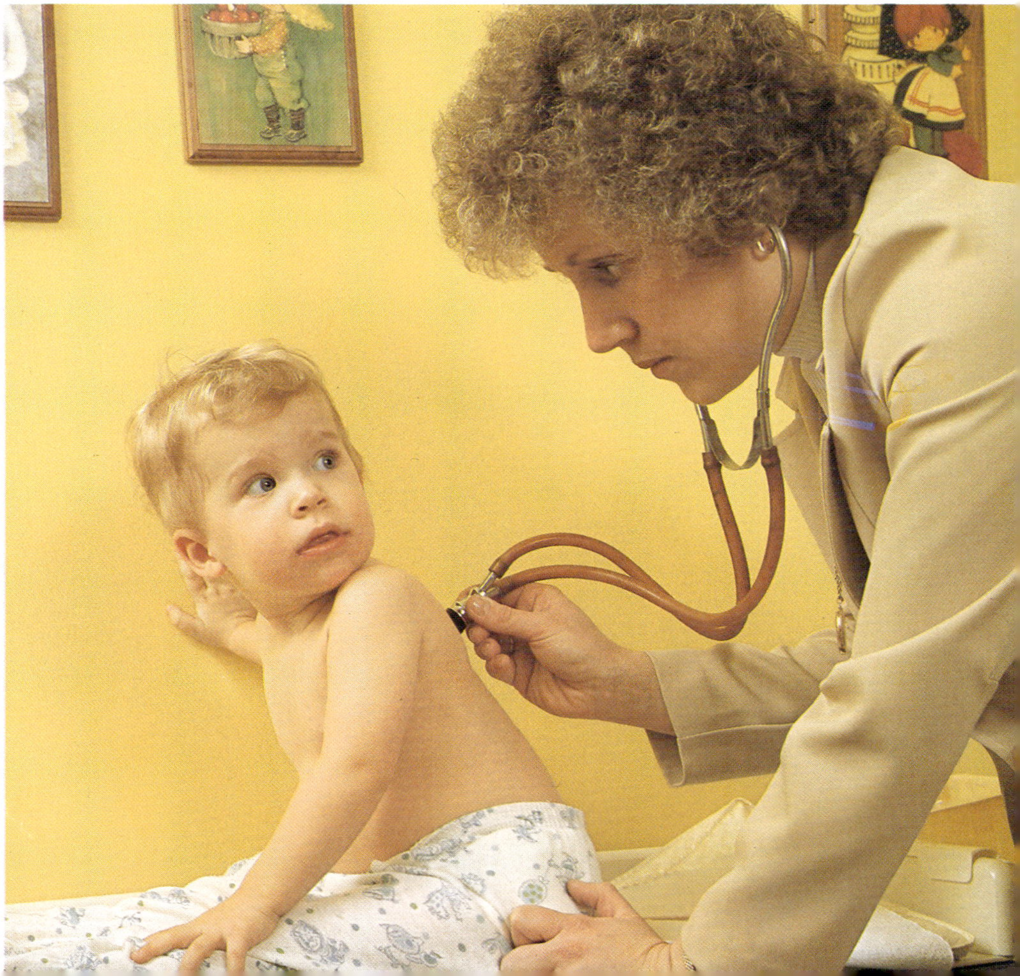

Stethoscopes are horribly cold, but they help this American doctor check that a baby's lungs are in good working order. A child living in damp conditions, for instance, may suffer from constant coughs or bronchitis. ▷

ALL ABOUT DOCTORS

There are all kinds of doctors. Some work in the community, and patients go to see them at their **clinics**. If people are very ill, a community-based doctor visits them at home. Other doctors treat patients who are ill in hospital, having tests done or waiting for an operation. There are doctors who are employed by factories to look after the workers, and doctors who work in school clinics giving children regular check-ups.

Doctors work in very different conditions. Some have modern clinics and use all the latest equipment. In contrast, some doctors who work in Africa or Asia may have to travel around, taking drugs and good advice to remote communities. Some doctors work in country villages; others in busy inner-city areas. The problems they face are different in each case, but the aim is the same – to prevent illness and to save lives.

Doctors may work alone or in health centres with other doctors, nurses, social workers and health visitors. A doctor may choose to specialize in one area of medicine. Your family doctor might send you to such a specialist for a second opinion. A special children's doctor is called a paediatrician.

Ambulances come in all shapes and sizes. This is an emergency helicopter in Los Angeles, USA. ▽

Doctors have to understand how the body works so that they recognize the **symptoms** of illness. They have to keep up-to-date with new medicines and drugs that are available and be able to explain to their patients how they work. They also have to be teachers – explaining to people how they can lead healthier lives and reduce their chances of becoming ill.

Most of all, doctors have to be clever detectives and good listeners. When they take our temperature, check our blood pressure or look into our ears, or eyes, or mouth, they are looking for clues to help them work out what might be wrong. What we tell them about ourselves helps their diagnosis. So to get the best care from a doctor, we have to learn about our bodies too. This means we can explain clearly what's wrong and understand the advice we are given. Keeping well is our responsibility too.

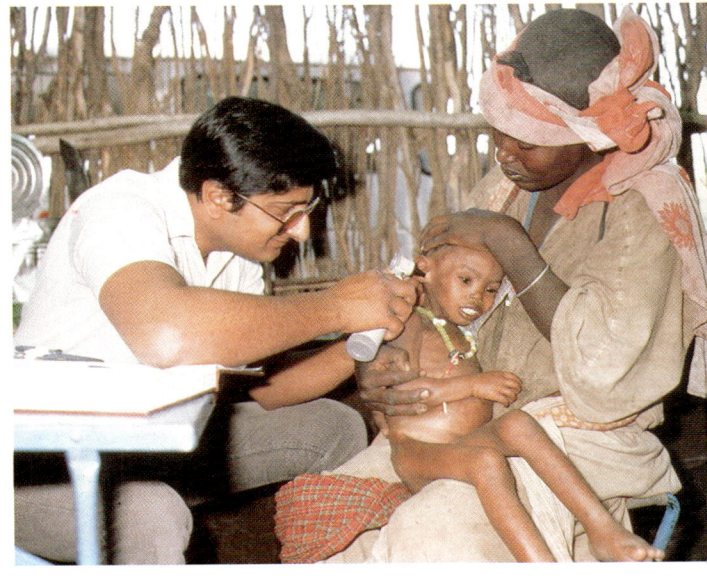

△ Doctors working in rural areas in developing countries, like Ethiopia, don't expect waiting rooms, smart desks and receptionists.

This Chinese doctor works at the Women's Hospital in Peking, where she advises patients on birth control. ▽

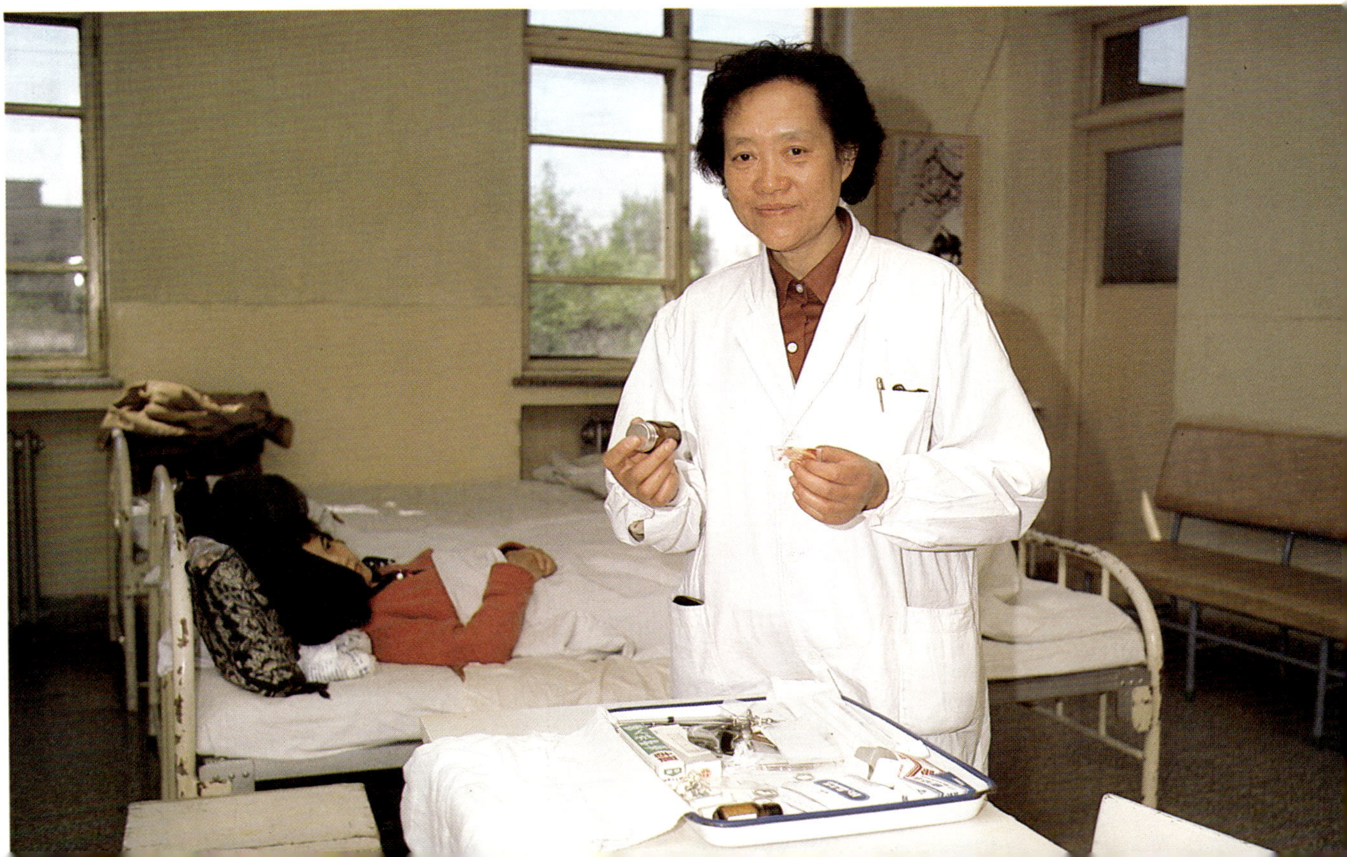

OTHER HEALTH WORKERS

△ **Volunteer nurses are a great help to understaffed hospitals and nurseries. This British girl is working in an orphanage in Bangladesh looking after ill babies there. Local women work there too.**

Wherever doctors work, they get together with other health workers. Each member of the team has very special skills. Health care is at its best when members of this team work together well, and when their patients are willing to help themselves.

Midwives look after pregnant women and help them when their babies are born. In poorer countries, health workers teach local women midwifery skills so that they know how to deliver a baby safely when there is no doctor nearby. They can then pass on their knowledge to other women.

Health visitors check up on new mothers and their babies, old people and anyone else who needs home visits. If necessary, they talk to doctors, midwives and social workers about a patient's problems.

Social workers help people who are having family problems. Perhaps someone in the household drinks too much alcohol, or the family cannot pay their rent and are very anxious, or an old person is at risk from the cold. The social worker gives advice and, if necessary, talks to a doctor or health visitor about these problems.

Opticians test people's eyes to see if they need glasses or contact lenses. In some parts of the world it is difficult to get glasses. When people who suffer from poor sight do get a pair of glasses through a health worker or a voluntary organization, it changes their lives.

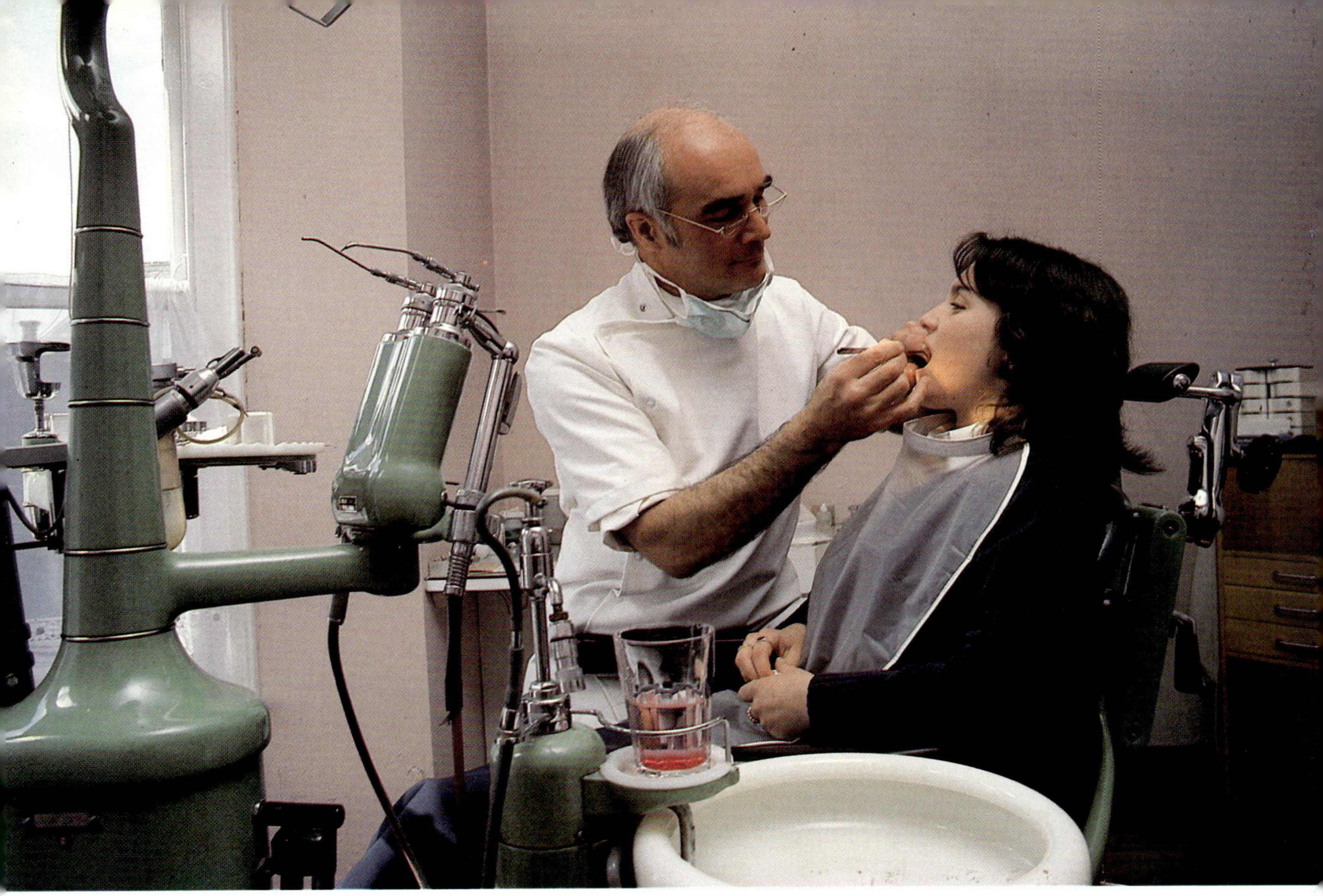

△ Tooth and gum disease have to be tackled by dentists. Many people in Western countries have bad teeth, and many people have false teeth in their twenties. The main reason for tooth decay is a diet containing too much sugar. Raw, crunchy vegetables are much better for our teeth.

△ Babies born before they are ready are called premature. Because they are so small they need special care 24 hours a day, and expensive equipment to help them breathe and take in food. Thanks to expert staff, like this nurse in Bahrain, far more premature babies now live when in the past they would have died. ▷

Chiropodists look after people's feet; physiotherapists help disabled people or accident victims exercise their limbs; dentists check teeth and gums. Tooth decay is a big problem in both rich and poor countries. Children quickly learn to enjoy sweets but not always how to clean their teeth properly!

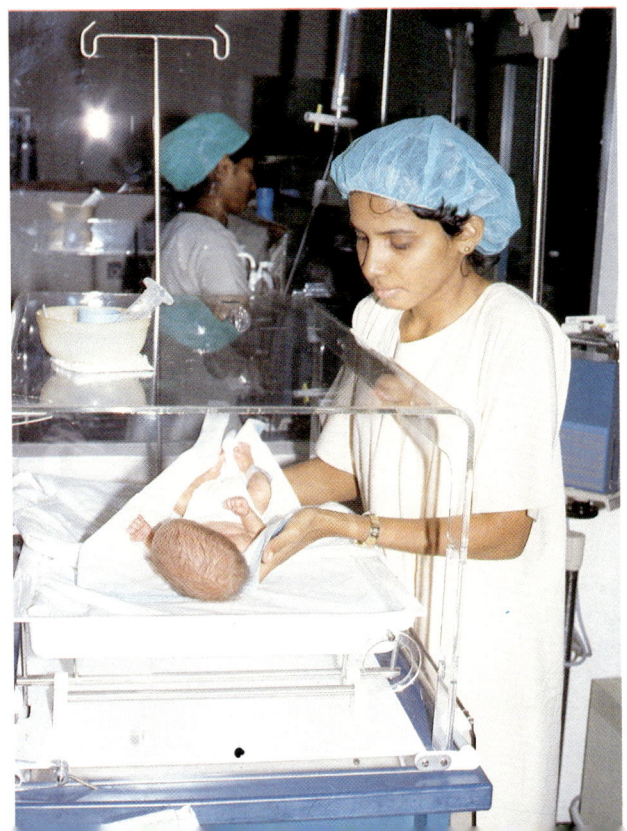

HOW HOSPITALS WORK

When people need an operation, or tests to see what is wrong with them, their doctors send them to hospital to see a surgeon or another specialist. They may pay only one visit, or they may have to stay there for several days. Most babies are born in hospital and elderly people can get special care there.

Hospitals come in all sizes, from big city teaching hospitals to smaller country hospitals and, in many parts of the world, field hospitals. These are set up on the spot to help a community.

General hospitals look after people with all kinds of illnesses; other hospitals concentrate on one problem such as eye operations, cancer, or children's diseases.

Most hospitals also have a Casualty Department, which looks after accident victims. All hospitals are organized by administrators who see that everything runs smoothly. Doctors and nurses look after the patients. Porters take patients from their beds in the wards to the **X-ray** department or to the operating theatre. There are laboratory technicians, cleaners, cooks and many others. Without this team, a hospital could not function properly.

In some countries, such as Britain, there are long waiting lists for some operations. The National Health Service needs more money to provide beds for the people who need them. If an old person needs a hip replacement operation because their own hip has worn out and is painful, they may have to wait up to three years. Many more hospital beds are needed for simple operations like these.

During times of famine in Africa or Asia, emergency hospitals, clinics and feeding centres are set up in rural areas, because permanent hospitals only exist in the bigger towns. Here, parents and children can be treated with drugs and antibiotics. Those suffering from malnutrition are given special high-calorie food until they are better.

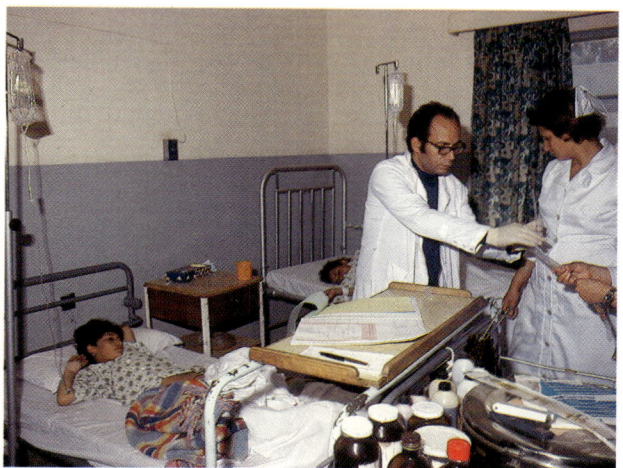

Some hospitals only deal with certain diseases, others are general hospitals which take in patients suffering from all kinds of illnesses. This is a general hospital in Kuwait. Doctors and nurses work together to make sure the patient gets the proper treatment and the best care. ▷

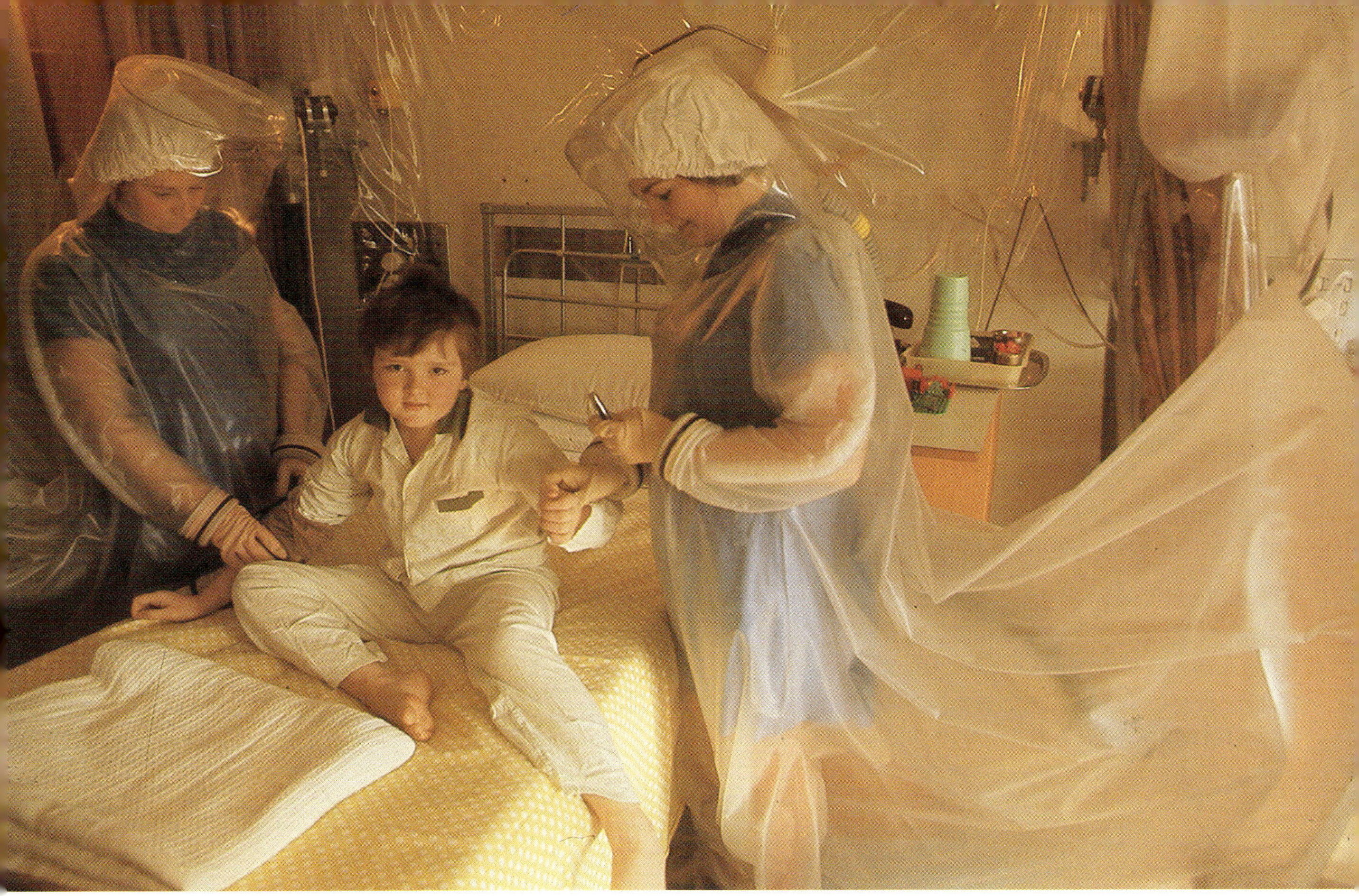

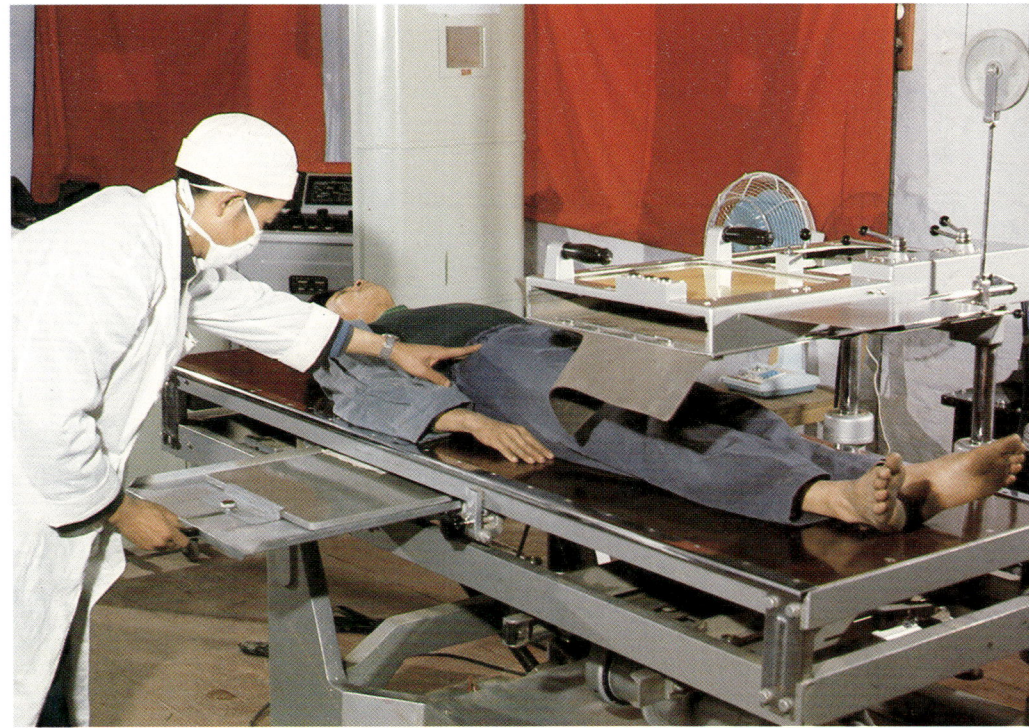

△ The Royal Marsden Hospital in London is a special hospital for cancer patients. This young boy is suffering fom leukaemia. The nurses are dressed in protective clothing to make sure they don't pass on any bacteria to the boy.

Big hospitals have many different departments. This patient in China is having an X-ray, where pictures are taken inside the body so that a doctor can see what is wrong. ▷

HELPING DISABLED CHILDREN

If your body works well and you can run, play games, see and hear clearly you are lucky. Some children cannot. They are disabled. They may have had a bad accident which means they can only get around in a wheelchair, or they may have been born like that. Other children may be blind or deaf, or both.

Disabled children need special care. Sometimes physiotherapy will help someone who has had polio to walk for the first time. Children with cerebral palsy can be treated, too. Others can learn to cope with their handicap, by living with children who are not disabled so they can help each other. Disabled children have to grow up, work and live in a world where most people can walk,

see and hear. That's very hard, and so we should give them plenty of help.

In Fiji, many children are born with cerebral palsy. Their limbs may be twisted and they have poor control of their movements. Health workers encourage the parents to bring them for physiotherapy. They also teach them simple exercises which they can do with their children at home. This helps a lot.

In a primary school in Khemisset, Morocco, doctors and physiotherapists help children who have had polio to walk again. Some need to have operations to straighten their legs. Others just need crutches or splints and lots of attention.

In Bath, England, the RNID (Royal

◁ **If, like this young girl, you cannot hear people speaking, or the wind blowing, or the TV, or the sound of laughter, life can be very lonely. Many charities help out. This is Riding for the Disabled.**

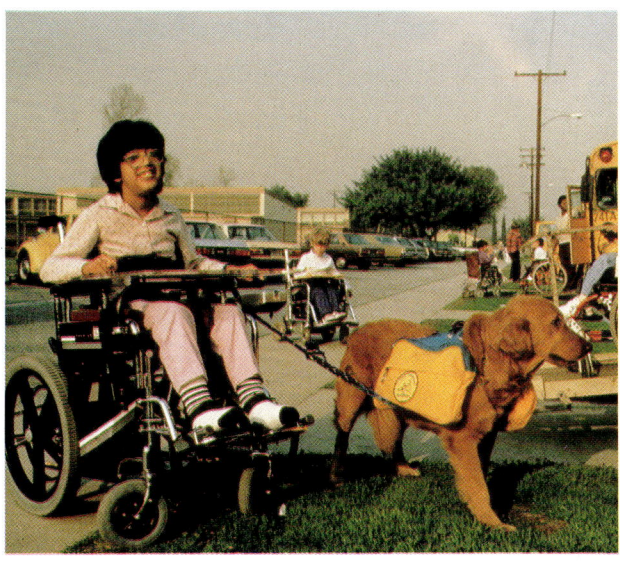

△ Handicapped children are just like other children: they like to play, chat, learn and enjoy themselves. These children in the United States are off on a day's outing.

The drug thalidomide caused babies to be born with deformities. But the children affected have found ways to cope. This little boy can play the electric organ with one hand. ▷

National Institute for the Deaf) runs a centre for young people who are deaf *and* blind. Before they come to the centre, they are trapped in a dark, silent world. They cannot speak because they have never heard anyone speak and so they cannot imitate how it is done. At the centre the trained helpers try and get through to these young people. They give them plenty of love. Soon they learn to speak and to read Braille – a language written in raised dots which blind people 'read' through touch. After a few months there, learning to look after themselves, many of these people are able to live in their own flats and do a useful job.

There are many voluntary organizations all over the world that help disabled children and adults.

MENTAL ILLNESS/HANDICAP

Some children are born mentally handicapped. Their brains are damaged and so they don't develop as they should. Such children are usually slower to learn skills such as reading, walking or talking. Children with **Down's Syndrome** are like this.

Like the body, the brain can also become ill. No one knows exactly why. Sometimes a serious injury to the head will cause mental illness or handicap. Epilepsy is a common illness which affects the brain. It can develop at any age and causes fits or convulsions, which can be controlled with drugs.

Other mental illnesses are caused by stress or anxiety; or perhaps by an imbalance of chemicals in the brain. Sometimes the effects become so strong that people need to see a **psychiatrist,** who will help them with drugs or other treatment, or a **psychotherapist** who will talk through their worries with them.

In many societies, mentally ill or handicapped people are often shut away in hospitals and special homes rather than accepted into their community. It is better for them if they live and mix with people who do not have their problems

and learn to look after themselves as much as possible. To do this successfully, they need help from people like social workers. Voluntary organizations have to work hard to change people's attitudes, so that they understand and accept people who are not like themselves.

Many handicapped children now go to ordinary schools, and have special lessons to help them learn. Adults recovering from an illness may live for a while in a hostel where social workers help them get used to coping again.

Two years ago, Oxfam helped set up a special day-centre in Roumieh, Lebanon, for mentally handicapped children living at home. In the Souf Refugee Camp in Jordan, young people have created a centre for twenty mentally and physically handicapped children. In Britain, Save the Children runs play buses and play centres for mentally handicapped children. Such schemes help people see they can live together, whatever problems they may have.

△ Mentally handicapped people need to be out and about in the community. At Minnowburn, Save the Children's youth farm in peaceful countryside near Belfast (Northern Ireland), children get away from troubled inner-city areas and get a chance to see how a farm works, to look after animals and to help grow vegetables.

Many children who are mentally handicapped go to ordinary schools, but there are also special schools and classes where they get individual attention to help them develop to their full potential. ▷

◁ Mentally handicapped children are often playful and very affectionate. They can also be quite a handful for their parents, who sometimes need a break from looking after them. This is a club for such children.

41

COMPLEMENTARY MEDICINE

Modern Western medicine uses manufactured drugs and **surgery** to treat illness. But there are other methods too. In China, for example, many people prefer to take traditional herbal medicines or have a course of acupuncture. An acupuncture patient has long, fine metal needles inserted into carefully selected points of the body to cure pain and various illnesses.

Until earlier this century, herbs were widely used in the West too. After all, penicillin, the first antibiotic, discovered by Sir Alexander Fleming in 1929, was not used to treat bacterial infections until

This Chinese man is having a major operation. He can't feel a thing because of the acupuncture needles in his ear. ▽

World War II (1939–45). Before that there was no quick way to cure a sore throat or a septic wound. For these and other minor problems, such as headaches, traditional remedies were used instead. In the nursery rhyme *Jack and Jill went up the Hill*, Jack fell down and broke his crown and had his head wrapped in 'vinegar and brown paper'. That was a traditional cure for headaches before aspirin was available. Today, medicine which does not use modern drugs is called 'alternative' (instead of) or 'complementary' (used together with conventional medicine). The most popular alternative medicines are acupuncture, herbal medicine and osteopathy, which is a combination of massage and the manipulation of joints.

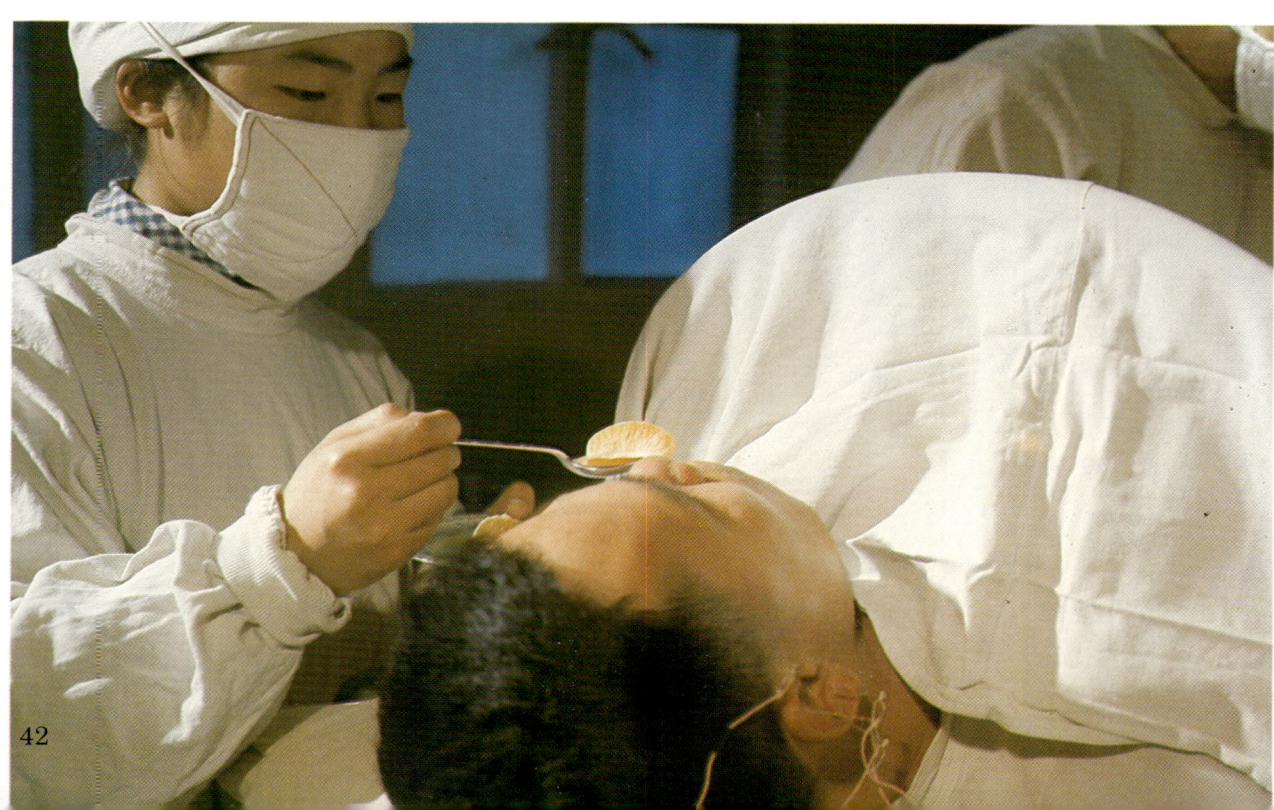

△ **In India 'health and strength' potion sellers are trusted members of the community.**

Traditional herbal medicine, like some of the medicines sold here in China, has recently become popular in Western countries. ▷

Western doctors working in developing countries often co-operate with local people trained in their own kind of medicine. In Ladakh, for instance, a mountainous province in North India, Save the Children health workers work with villagers practising traditional Amchi medicine. Amchis obtain many of their medicines from local herbs and plants, or crushed rocks. Nowadays, they are also using antibiotics, measles vaccine and antiseptic ointments. This truly is complementary medicine, combining the best of both kinds of treatment.

GLOSSARY

Antibiotics Medicines which treat illnesses caused by bacteria (germs).

Blood pressure The pressure put on the arteries by the blood, which is pumped round the body by the heart. High blood pressure, caused mostly by a high-fat diet, is dangerous and can lead to heart disease.

Clinics Centres for health care where doctors, nurses and other health workers see patients.

Contaminated Crops which have been poisoned with chemical sprays and are not fit to eat are called contaminated. The water in rivers and lakes, or the sea can become contaminated if sewage or industrial waste is dumped there.

Contraception Pills or special devices which prevent a woman becoming pregnant.

Dehydration A slow process where the body dries out because there is not enough water to drink.

Developing countries Poorer countries which do not yet have the housing, work opportunities, education or health care that rich countries, or **developed countries**, take for granted.

Down's Syndrome Babies born with this are mentally backward and very vulnerable to infection.

Epidemic A disease which spreads quickly and infects a large number of people in an area or country.

Haemophilia A physical condition where the blood does not clot properly, so that small cuts and bruises can be very dangerous because the bleeding does not stop.

Heart transplant A life-saving operation to give a new heart to a patient whose own heart is diseased.

Immune system The white blood cells in our bodies which fight disease and infection and so keep us healthy.

Junk food Food which is unhealthy because it contains too much fat or additives, such as flavourings, preservatives and colouring.

Malnutrition When a person becomes ill because they are not eating enough food or the wrong kind of food.

Pollution The result when chemicals, oil, rubbish or sewage are allowed to spoil our seas, rivers and landscape.

Prescription charges Money British people pay for medicines the doctor decides they should have.

Psychiatrist A specialist who treats mental illness.

Psychotherapist A person who counsels anyone suffering from depression, anxiety and other mental problems.

Radiation sickness Vomiting, headaches, hair loss and other problems which may be fatal. It is caused by fall-out from nuclear bombs, and leaks from nuclear power stations.

Refugees People who have to leave their homes because of war or famine and move to a strange country or district.

Reservoirs Man-made lakes used for storing water.

Social security Money and other help given to people by the government if they cannot provide for themselves.

Stress Feelings caused by being anxious or depressed about our problems or by overwork. Stress can make other illnesses worse.

Surgery Treatment for an illness by an operation.

Symptoms The signs that a person is ill. A blocked-up nose, for example, is a symptom of a cold.

Vaccine A treatment which prevents someone getting a particular disease.

Voluntary organization An agency which gets much of its money through donations from the general public, and which gives help to people in need. Save the Children, Oxfam, War on Want, Christian Aid are all voluntary organizations.

X-ray A special photograph which shows the inside of the body.

44

TEACHERS' NOTES

Younger children respond well to the idea of looking after their own bodies. Research done by the Health Education Council (before it was disbanded early in 1987) shows that up to about the age of 12, health education is successful. The dangers of smoking, eating too much fat and too many sweets, the importance of looking after teeth, hair and taking exercise, all make sense to children.

It is only if these aspects of 'self-health' are left until puberty that other, more pressing, concerns, such as boyfriends, and peer-group pressure, drive an adolescent constantly towards the take-away fish and chip shop and the tobacconist. By that time it could be too late to encourage them to be their own health watchdogs.

There are many books available for primary schoolchildren on how the body works which can be used for project work on all kinds of topics dealing with health and disease.

Practical first aid, involving role play, is also a favourite classroom activity. The children can be encouraged to make their own wallcharts on the kiss of life, for instance, or making a sling for a broken arm, as well as good nutrition.

Similarly, children are easily motivated to think about the plight of children in less developed countries. It is important for them to understand the problems. Encouraging them to write poems, devise short plays or dances on the themes of 'water', 'poverty', 'hunger', 'thirst' will help them to make use of source material you have in the classroom.

At the same time, it's a good idea to emphasize the more positive aspects of life in poorer countries and not to reinforce the idea of 'them' and 'us'. Explain that men, women and children living in remote villages need to know more about basic health care and medicines. Whereas we have recourse to doctors and hospitals when we become ill, they may only have their common sense to rely on. So a practical project showing the techniques involved in, say, making a water pump or digging a well, will make these facts clearer.

The *Child-to-Child* project described on page 28 of this book (and see Books to Read) could be used to show just how much responsibility poorer children must take for the health and well-being of themselves and their families. They might like to try some health education in their own homes.

A look at alternative medicine, nineteenth-century herbal recipes – they could be made up at school – witch doctor magic, a discussion of faith healing, perhaps poems and stories written by mentally handicapped people, the artistic achievements of blind or disabled children, can all help to extend a child's understanding of the wider aspects of health and sickness in a complex society.

PICTURE CREDITS

USEFUL ADDRESSES

Many organizations produce useful teachers' materials on health in developed and developing countries:

The Health Education Authority, 78 New Oxford Street, London WC1, produces a wealth of leaflets and colourful posters aimed at adults and children on a variety of health topics.

ASH, Action for Smoking and Health, 5/11 Mortimer Street W1N 7RH.

Drugs Information and Advisory Service Ltd, 11 Cowbridge Road East, Canton, Cardiff.

British Homeopathic Association, 27a Devonshire Street, London W1N 1RJ.

British Acupuncture Association, 37 Peter Street, Manchester M2 5QD.

British Dental Health Foundation, 26 Ravensdale Avenue, London N12 9HS.

National Society for the Prevention of Cruelty to Children (NSPCC), 1 Riding House Street, London W1P 8AA.

National Children's Bureau, 8 Wakeley Street, London EC1V 7QE.

MENCAP (Society for Mentally Handicapped Children and Adults), 123 Golden Lane, London EC1Y 0RT.

UNICEF, 55–56 Lincoln's Inn Fields, London WC2A 3NB.

Save the Children, Mary Datchelor House, 17 Grove Lane, London SE5 8RD, produce an activity pack for schools called *Getting Better* and can help with slides and other material.

Oxfam, Oxfam House 274 Banbury Road, Oxford OX2 7DZ. Write for details of their schools' material and useful books. Or visit their library.

Christian Aid, P.O. Box 1, London SW9 8BH.

Catholic Fund for Overseas Development, 2 Garden Close, Stockwell Road, London SW9 9TY.

Council for Education in World Citizenship, Seymour Mews House, Seymour Mews, London W1H 9PE.

Commonwealth Institute, Kensington High Street, London W8 8NQ.

Information Department, **Overseas Development Administration**, Room E920, Eland House, Stag Place, London SW1.

The Centre for World Development Education, Regent's College, Inner Circle, Regent's Park, London NW1 4NS also has good material, books, leaflets, slides and activity packs. Some of these are detailed on page 47. Write for a catalogue.

Institute of Child Health, 30 Guildford Street, London WC1N 1EH. The library here has a large collection of country files that can be consulted and a series of slide packs for loan to schools.

College of Health, Association for Consumer Research, 14 Buckingham Street, London WC2N 6DS.

Hampshire Development Education Centre, Mid Hants Teachers' Centre, Elm Road, Winchester, Hants SO22 5AG. Write to them for *The World Tomorrow*, a series of development topics for children.

BOOKS TO READ

FOR YOUNGER READERS

Health and Drugs, by Dorothy Baldwin (Wayland, 1987).

Health and Exercise, by Dorothy Baldwin (Wayland, 1987).

Health and Feelings, by Dorothy Baldwin (Wayland, 1987).

Health and Food, by Dorothy Baldwin (Wayland, 1987).

Health and Friends, by Dorothy Baldwin (Wayland, 1987).

Health and Hygiene, by Dorothy Baldwin (Wayland, 1987).

Junior Body Machine: How the human body works Consulting Editor Christiaan Barnard(Kestrel Books).

Just look at Health by Brian Ward (Macdonald, 1986).

The Young Scientist Book of Medicine, Doctors and Health by Pam Beasant (Usborne, 1985).

FOR OLDER READERS

Food or Famine by Christopher Gibb (Wayland, 1987).

The Politics of Food by Martin Schultz (Wayland, 1981).

World Health, by Janie Hampton (Wayland, 1987).

The World Health Organization by Peter Corrigan (Wayland, 1979).

FOR TEACHERS

Teaching Development Issues (Manchester DEP, 1986). Series of seven books giving support to teachers. Section 4 is **Health** (Also available from CWDE, order no. H-67).

Teaching World Studies an introduction to global perspectives in the curriculum. Edited by Hicks and Townley (Longman, 1982). Also available from CWDE, order no. H-57.

World Studies 8–13 A Teacher's Handbook by Simon Fisher and David Hicks (Oliver and Boyd, 1986). Part 1: Curriculum Planning. Part 2: Classroom Activities. Part 3: In-Service Ideas.

The following materials are a selection available from the Centre for World Development Education (see Useful Addresses). Write for a full catalogue, or write to the organizations which publish them.

Child-to-Child, Health Care in Kenya Oxfam Jigsaw booklet for middle schools. Order no. B-130.

Child Survival: Four Key Elements UNICEF wallchart. Order no. W-43.

Disease Christian Aid 'Caring' worksheet for primary schools. Order no. L-153.

Health, Environment, Water, Children and other titles. Cartoonsheet Discussion Starters (available singly or in bulk for class use at a discount).

Health for All Christian Aid illustrated topic sheet for secondary schools. Order no. L-145.

Healthy, Wealthy and Wise? Oxfam Pictorial Discussion Sheets. Illustrated. Secondary schools. Order no. L-19.

Index